100 KEYS

TO

WOODSHOP SAFETY

Alan and Gill Bridgewater

BETTERWAY BOOKS

A QUARTO BOOK

Copyright © 1996
Quarto Inc.

First Published in
the U.S.A. by
Betterway Books,
an imprint of
F & W Publications, Inc.
1507 Dana Avenue
Cincinnati, Ohio 45207
(800) 289 0963

ISBN 1-55870-430-2

This book was
designed and produced
by Quarto Publishing plc
The Old Brewery
6 Blundell Street
London N7 9BH

Contents

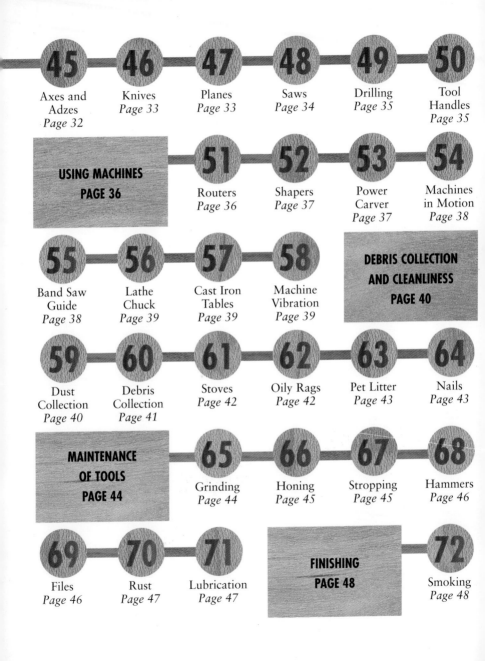

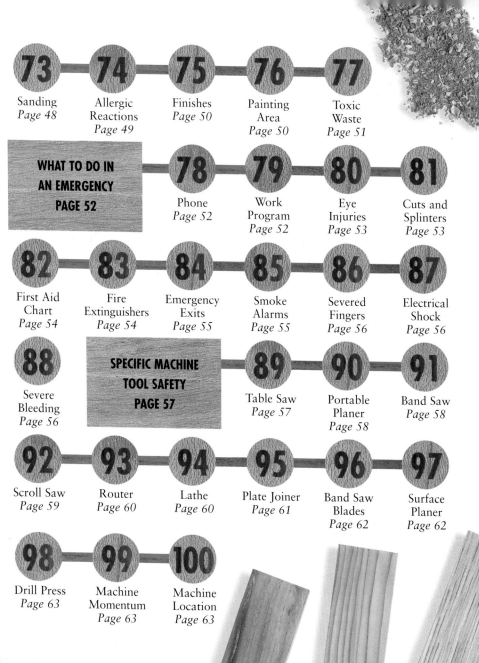

INTRODUCTION

SOMETIMES, IN THE COZY, quiet, dust-free corner of my woodshop, at the end of the day when the sun's gone down, I take one of my pieces of woodwork, shut my eyes, and run my finger tips over the joints and the textures. It's a great feeling to sit there, in my old armchair, to follow the knots and the grain, to relive the hours spent cutting the sap-sweet, butter-smooth wood, and then to open my eyes and wander around the woodshop, and to know that the furniture, turnings, carvings and toys have been painstakingly worked with my own two hands. Woodworking is a uniquely creative experience that should not be missed. Okay, so we all know about the delights of woodworking, but what about the nightmare woodshops, where the workers are dogged by cut and crushed fingers, sneezing and wheezing, strained muscles, and all the other horrors that haunt the craft. I'm sure you know what I mean – the woodshops that are knee-deep in shavings, with frayed power cords snaking across the floor, and dust-laden cobwebs dripping from the ceiling, where the wheezing workers eat, drink and smoke amidst a morass of dust, debris, tools, noise and fumes. Yuck! Is it any wonder that such woodshops are inefficient, with the stressed workers always bemoaning their bad luck!

Stop a moment and take a good long look at your hands. It's wonderful, isn't it – to think that your finger tips are so sensitive that they can feel degrees of texture too slight to be seen with the naked eye? Unfortunately, the grim and grisly reality of working in a sloppy, badly run woodshop is that, before you can say choppers-whizzers-cutters-and-slashers, you can lose a finger, or damage your eyes or at the very least receive a nasty gash. Move your hands and ask yourself: Where would I be without those super-sensory digits?

In recent woodshop safety surveys the real surprise is, not that woodworking tools are responsible for most hand-related industrial accidents, but rather that these same reports also declare that virtually all woodworking accidents could so easily be prevented. Still, the nightmare continues.

But enough of the agony and ecstasy of woodworking. I make no excuse for the purple shock-horror imagery, because the good news is that most woodshop problems can be corrected simply by changing routines and procedures and/or by rethinking the way your tools and machines are organized. For example, since most power tool and machine accidents result from repetition, fatigue, overconfidence and inexperience – or a combination of all four – all you really need to do is to be aware of the problems and risks and then follow-through with a self-help program. Many safety aids can be made and up-and-running in just a few minutes. Better yet, you don't have to spend a lot on sophisticated widgets; all you need to do – as my grandpa used to say – is read some, learn some, and act some.

So there you go. If you want to achieve an optimum woodshop environment, and cut down on the hazards and health risks, and in the doing smooth out your woodshop operation and generally maximize your woodworking efficiency and creativity, then just keep reading. We show you how.

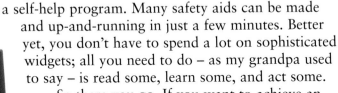

SAFE WOODSHOP SETUP

Woodworking – carving, turning, furniture making, toymaking, and all the rest – is a wonderfully joyous and therapeutic activity, but only if the woodshop is clean, well organized and, above all, safe. The following primary pointers will help you create a positive, healthy, user-friendly woodshop environment.

1 **FLOOR SPACE** Machines must be located so that there is room to maneuver. There needs to be plenty of all-round space, so that the workpiece can be freely fed into the machine at one side and extracted at the other. The amount of space should relate to the size and type of work produced. For example, the space needed to make small toys will obviously be less than that needed to make furniture. As lumber always comes in lengths, and as the procedures necessarily involve walking from one machine to another – and all manner of bending, stretching, and lifting activities besides – it is best to aim for as much space as possible.

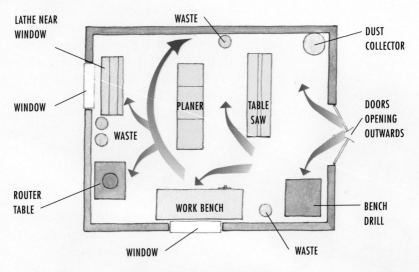

Labels: LATHE NEAR WINDOW, WASTE, DUST COLLECTOR, WINDOW, PLANER, TABLE SAW, DOORS OPENING OUTWARDS, WASTE, ROUTER TABLE, WORK BENCH, BENCH DRILL, WINDOW, WASTE

Arrange the worktables and machines so that you are able to move freely from one to another.

WALL SURFACES

Clean, bright walls make for a safe working environment. Though your woodshop might well be built of anything from concrete block to wood framing, the actual interior wall surfaces need to be smooth, light in color, fire resistant, dry, and generally easy to clean and maintain. Most woodworkers favor white painted plasterboard or plywood for the walls and ceilings. Fiber or cork bulletin boards are useful for displaying designs, telephone numbers, timetables and the like; and battened areas are good for shelving. Some woodworkers find sections of pegboard useful for hanging up tools, but make sure peg hooks are secure so they don't come out when you pull down a tool.

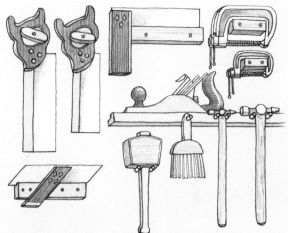

Organize your tool board with pegs and brackets so that everything is in full view and easy to reach.

Store all your heavy items on shelves and in pigeon holes.

SAFE WOODSHOP SETUP

Cushion-back vinyl

Untreated cork tile

Rubber tile

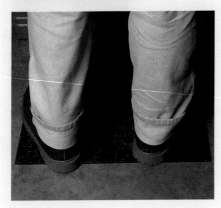

FLOOR SURFACES The floor surface should be stable, dry, hard wearing, fireproof, easy to clean, pleasing to the eye, and non trip-and-slip. Most woodworkers favor a solid concrete slab, with selected areas covered with various secondary finishes. Depending upon your personal likes and needs – and of course the size of your bank balance – a concrete floor might be painted, or covered with industrial grade sheeting, rubber/cork/vinyl-tiled or even finished with strip hardwood. If you work for extended periods of time standing in one place, such as at a workbench or lathe, you may want to put down a rubber anti-fatigue mat.

BE WARNED – Steps, slight level changes, and slopes are a bad idea! – sooner or later you are going to trip over them. Worse yet, such features, break up the useful floor area, restrict tool, machine and bench usage and make sweeping and wet mopping even more of a chore.

A rubber mat doubles up as an anti-fatigue surface and an anti-slip surface.

ANTI-SLIP SURFACES A considerable number of woodshop accidents are caused by slippery floors. If you are at all worried about slipping – say in front of a hazardous machine like a lathe – you might consider creating anti-slip surfaces. A swift money-saver is to paint selected areas with a rubber type adhesive, sprinkle sharp, dry sand over the adhesive, wait for it to cure, and then sweep up the excess sand.

5 **QUIET CORNER** Knowing that fatigue is dangerous, it's a good idea to have a small area set aside for designing, contemplation, and rest. If you like this notion, you could have the area carpeted and screened off from noise, dust and debris. Save money by fitting this area out with bits and pieces salvaged from your home – such items as a little table for drawing, a comfortable armchair, and a cabinet for storing your drawing equipment. Don't forget the coffee pot!

6 **AIR AND WINDOWS** For health and safety's sake, clean air is a must. Your woodshop must be ventilated with opening windows and/or an air filter system. Planning regulations generally recommend that the area of opening windows must equal 20% of the total floor area. If you need to remove fumes and stale air, then you will require a positive-pressure ventilation system (PPV). A good, swift money-saver, is to set a fan outside the workshop in such a way that fast-moving air tracks directly into the workshop and out through windows and vents. Or what better, on a summer's day, than to throw the doors open and work with plenty of sunshine and fresh air. In winter, you'll save on heating bills by keeping windows closed and using a ceiling-mounted recirculating air filter.

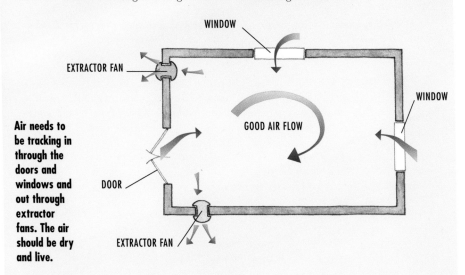

WINDOW

EXTRACTOR FAN

WINDOW

GOOD AIR FLOW

Air needs to be tracking in through the doors and windows and out through extractor fans. The air should be dry and live.

DOOR

EXTRACTOR FAN

SAFE WOODSHOP SETUP

34 inches

Traditional bench for a man: 34 inches.

26-30 inches

Traditional bench for a woman or youth: 26-30 inches.

32-33½ inches

Stand-up counter: 32-33½ inches.

7 **WORKING HEIGHT** Making do with a work surface that is at the wrong height is a bad idea: It will make your back ache, and it will put you at risk when you variously reach or stoop to work at a machine. A work surface – whether it is a work bench, desk, or stand-up counter – must be at the correct working height. The height of a work surface should be adjusted to suit individual needs, but aim for a height that minimizes stretch and shoulder hunch. The illustrated heights are a guide.

15-18 inches

Sit-on donkey or shaving horse: 15-18 inches.

8 **SHELVES AND STORAGE** Safe and efficient workshops have one common feature: lots of well-planned storage – fixed shelves, freestanding units with movable shelving, built-in wall cabinets, under-bench shelves and cabinets and so on. If you stay with the following safe location pointers, you won't go far wrong:

- Site the shelves and cabinets so that they are easy to reach and so that you don't have to stretch over a machine.
- Make sure shelves don't overhang machines like lathes – you don't want a tool to slide off a shelf and onto a fast-spinning cutter blade or chuck.
- Make sure shelves are fixed to a stable surface so that they don't vibrate when the machines are powered up.

ELECTRICAL SAFETY

Though we are all familiar with electric lights and power outlets, it is this very familiarity that causes safety problems. The following guides and tips will enable you to run a safe and efficient woodshop. BE WARNED – With electricity, ignorance is more than dangerous – it is a potential killer! If you have any doubts about the following tips, or the condition and potential of your electrical system, then have it checked out by a qualified electrician.

9

LIGHTING Ideally, all machines and work surfaces need to be positioned so that there is a well-balanced mix of natural and artificial light. In windowless shops, take extra care to provide adequate lighting without shadows. Specific tasks, and left and right handedness might well call for additional lighting options. The overall goal is a lighting level that eliminates glare and hard shadow. For example, with a lathe positioned in front of a window, and with ceiling lights at top-center, you might also require additional flex-armed lamps to your right, to throw light directly into the point-of-cut.

A badly lighted lathe is dangerous.

Position a lamp for side light so that the working area is free from glare and shadow.

ELECTRICAL SAFETY

10 **WIRING** All electrical wiring must be in good condition and properly insulated. If the installation is old – say about 25-30 years – then it really needs replacing with modern insulated cable. It's best to check local building and electrical code requirements and have the system wired by a qualified electrician. Work with the electrician to locate wiring and outlets convenient to work areas with adequate provisions for both 110-volt and 220-volt circuits as needed. If your local code allows, you may want to consider locating cables in surface mounted raceways. Then, not only can you swiftly and safely modify the system to meet your changing needs, but better yet, you won't have problems when you want to mount shelves and machines on the walls. You may also consider ceiling-mounted wiring for some machines.

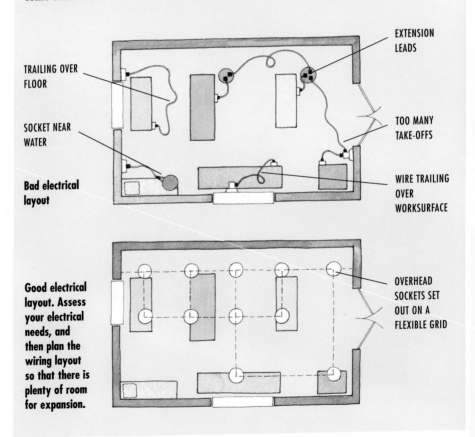

EXTENSION LEADS

TRAILING OVER FLOOR

SOCKET NEAR WATER

Bad electrical layout

TOO MANY TAKE-OFFS

WIRE TRAILING OVER WORKSURFACE

Good electrical layout. Assess your electrical needs, and then plan the wiring layout so that there is plenty of room for expansion.

OVERHEAD SOCKETS SET OUT ON A FLEXIBLE GRID

11 **FLUORESCENT LIGHTING** The most common and by far the most economical shop lights are fluorescent fixtures. They are many times more efficient than incandescent bulbs. They are also available in full-spectrum forms that simulate natural lighting. That's especially helpful for finishing where color-matching is important. For those who complain that fluorescents' flickering gives them headaches, non-flickering alternatives are also available, or you can stick with conventional lighting.

12 **CIRCUIT BREAKERS** You don't need to understand how circuit breakers work, but suffice it to say they are the primary way of protecting you and the machines from electrical damage. In use, the circuit breaker literally breaks the circuit when the system is overloaded, or when you do something stupid like banging a nail through a cable. Have your electrician make sure your circuit breakers and electrical service are adequate to your needs. Most homes typically have 100 to 200-amp electrical service. If you have an old system with fuses instead of circuit breakers, consider replacing it. Adding a ground-fault circuit interruptor (GFCI) provides extra protection against short circuits and may be required by building codes in such installations as basement shops.

13 **JUNCTION BOX** The junction box houses the main switch and the circuit breakers or fuses for the whole electrical installation. As the unit is usually the first port of call when the power fails, or when there is a machine emergency, it follows that it needs to be located within easy reach. If your present unit is high up on the wall, in a dark cupboard or even outside, then consider having it relocated by a competent electrician.

14 **EXTENSION CORDS** In the context of woodshop safety, extension cords are always a bad idea! If they are snaking across the floor or over work surfaces, then sooner or later you are going to trip over them, and/or damage them with a sharp tool or a heavy piece of equipment. Furthermore, longer cords steal power from electric motors and may result in premature motor failure. If you have no choice but to use an extension cord, be sure to have a portable circuit breaker in-line. Use the shortest cord and the largest wire gauge available to minimize voltage drop.

OUTLETS AND SWITCHES Isn't it always the case that electrical outlets seem to be on the wrong side of the room! If you are at the planning stage, then go for as many outlets as possible – one every four to six feet along walls is not outrageous. It's a good super-safe idea to have an emergency punch button or trip wire switch with every machine. Fit cord-pull switches near sinks and over benches. Many woodworkers eliminate the where-to-have-the-cable problem, by having the switches and sockets organized so that they are suspended from the ceiling. Floor-mounted receptacles also work well for stationary machines.

The plug-still-in scenario is an accident just waiting to happen!

For optimum safety, pull out the plug and keep it in full view.

UNPLUG FOR SAFETY One of the most common causes of accidents is not taking the little extra time to do something the safe way. This is particularly true when it comes to electricity and machine set-ups. When it comes time to change a bit or a blade, unplug the machine first. Don't take a chance on it accidentally getting switched on with your hand in the works. The best method whenever working on a machine is not only to unplug it but to keep the power cord end in plain view, so you know it's unplugged.

17

HEATING Cold fingers and toes equal slow response times; your woodshop needs adequate heating. Oil-fired, electric and wood heat systems similar to those used in homes are all woodshop options. Bear in mind that, whatever system you use, the object of the heating is two-fold – to keep you warm and to eliminate the condensation that does so much damage to tools and machines. If you must use temporary space heaters, always avoid gas and kerosene heaters that give off water vapor and also present a potential carbon monoxide hazard in a closed shop.

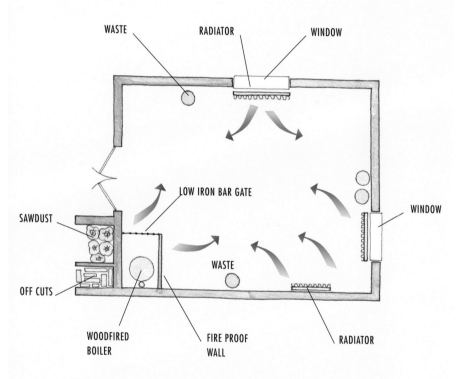

WASTE   RADIATOR   WINDOW

LOW IRON BAR GATE

SAWDUST

WINDOW

WASTE

OFF CUTS

WOODFIRED BOILER   FIRE PROOF WALL   RADIATOR

A ground floor workshop. An enclosed woodburning stove with a boiler and radiators is an all-round winner – it gets rid of your waste and keeps you warm. Plan the layout so that there is an adequate fuel storage area.

PEOPLE SAFETY – FOR YOU AND VISITORS

Of course, you may know how to look after yourself in a woodshop, but what about visitors? Woodshops are by their very nature both dynamic and dangerous, presenting extra hazards for children, pets, family, and curious friends. That's all the more reason why the woodshop environment needs to be clean, safe, tidy, and secure. If your shop is safer for visitors, it will be safer for you.

18 ACCESS

Although all the doors and windows need to have locks and catches, on no account should you ever be locked in, or, say, the kids and family locked out. If you want to work without interruption, then put a notice outside the door. If you have a choice (check your local building code), make sure that all the doors open outwards and are fitted with catches that allow you to push your way out in case of an emergency. Ideally you need two doors, so that there is always at least one clear and convenient exit.

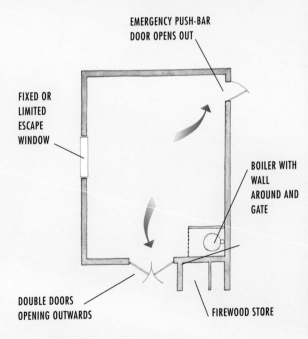

EMERGENCY PUSH-BAR DOOR OPENS OUT

FIXED OR LIMITED ESCAPE WINDOW

BOILER WITH WALL AROUND AND GATE

DOUBLE DOORS OPENING OUTWARDS

FIREWOOD STORE

A ground floor woodshop with minimum window openings. Every woodshop needs two emergency exists – either two doors, or a door and an opening widow.

VISITING CHILDREN As most kids enjoy woodworking, it is important that they be encouraged to watch and participate, but do emphasize control and care. Allow no more than three at a time in the shop. Visiting kids should first be checked out to make sure that they are fitted correctly with appropriate clothing and safety equipment, such as safety glasses, hearing protection and a respirator as necessary. First sit them down at a safe watching distance, then show them on a hands-on basis how to perform such-and-such a task. Keep sharp-edged tools as far back on the bench as possible, and the floor must not be cluttered with sharp-edged machinery. As kids are fascinated by machines and knives, always make sure that all doors and windows are locked when the workshop is not in use.

TOXIC MATERIALS Many woodshop materials are inherently unsafe – some types of exotic wood, all wood dust, chemicals like acetone, methylene chloride, various paints, adhesives and varnishes, and so on. When you are using and storing products, be sure to read the manufacturer's guidelines, and then act accordingly. For most chemical products like paint and adhesives you can contact the manufacturer to obtain the Material Safety and Data Sheets (MSDS) that explain proper use and hazards. Some woods are toxic, so ask yourself before using a new wood: Is it used locally? Is it a traditional choice for the task you have in mind? If in doubt, seek the advice of a specialist supplier.

IRRITANT

POWER LOCK-UP Many modern woodworking machines – lathes, band saws and such like – are fitted with a lock and/or have a removable on/off switch. The idea is that you can disable the machine when you are absent from the workshop.

Disable the machine by fitting a lock.

22 PAINT LEFTOVERS Yes, your grandpa's old leftover paint might still be in good condition, and yes, it will give a wonderfully glossy, hard-wearing finish, but of course, it will almost certainly contain highly poisonous lead! Then again, many old powder pigments contain such delights as arsenic and antimony – both poisonous! On the premise that many old products are either toxic or corrosive – or both – the best advice is to dispose of them properly. Check with local officials about legal disposal of small quantities of hazardous waste.

24 PRODUCT LIABILITY If you have it in mind to sell your work – toys, furniture, turned bowls, or whatever – then you are legally obligated to ensure the work is safe, and fitting the purpose for which it was designed. For example, if you make a bedside lamp for sale, then it is your responsibility to make sure that everything about the lamp is safe – the finish, the structure, the wood type, and the electrical fittings. If you have doubts, make contact with local consumer groups and advisory bodies.

BE WARNED – Ignorance is no excuse!

23 CHILD-SAFE TOYS Traditional wooden toys are great fun! – woodworkers like making them, and kids like playing with them. That said, you do have to bear in mind that finger-sticky toddlers are almost certainly going to be licking and sucking the toy, and generally doing their best to push it up their noses and in their ears – if not worse! You MUST make sure that the wood is splinter free, non-toxic and otherwise safe.

PERSONAL PROTECTION AND SAFETY CHECK LISTS

With the increased use of woodworking machinery, it is becoming more and more important that woodworkers follow through a program of positive safety. You need to run through a general safety check before you switch on machines, and you need to wear suitable protective clothing. The following guides will help you to keep your body out of harm's way.

25

KNOW YOUR MACHINE

Having first read the owner's manual and made yourself familiar with the machine's function, you must always run through a pre-power check list. Ask yourself such questions as: Are the guards down? Does the on/off switch work? Are the tools out of harm's way? and so on. Being mindful that familiarity leads to all manner of potentially dangerous short-cuts, you should pin the check list up on the wall near the machine.

Lower the guard for optimum clearance.

Always test switches before getting down to work.

Adjust the band saw guard so that there is about ½ inch clearance.

Set the drill press guard so that the chuck is covered but still in clear view.

KEYS AND WRENCHES Before you switch on, make sure that you have removed chuck keys and Allen wrenches. This is particularly important in the context of lathe and drill press chuck keys. If you can't remember to remove the key before switch-on, then make a huge ring for the key out of plywood or colored wire – so big that it's an unavoidable hindrance – or simply chain the key to the machine base.

CLEAN MACHINES Keep the area in and around the machine clean and uncluttered. Dust, oil and debris invite accidents. Wood shavings are particularly dangerous in that they gradually polish the floor to a shiny finish.

Polish the work bed so as to reduce potentially dangerous friction.

Clean up the dust and debris as soon as the job is complete.

28 **VISITING CHILDREN** Always welcome your children in the shop, but provide them with safety goggles, and sit them down at a safe distance. Use this quality time to educate the kids in the safe use of the machines. Bear in mind – before switching on portable planers and such like – that the waste wood is invariably spat out at child's-eye level.

Never leave the key in the lathe chuck.

29 **CHILDPROOF** Children are always curious, so be sure to lock up the workshop, and remove start-up keys. If you have a home woodshop and kids, then you must follow a program of positive education and protection. If your kids are at the got-to-give-it-a-try stage, then fit padlocks to all the machines.

Use a small brush to clean out the "stop" and "guard" channels.

PERSONAL PROTECTION AND SAFETY CHECK LISTS

30 WOODSHOP CLOTHING

Many accidents have to do with clothing and such getting dragged into the machines. Make sure that you are dressed appropriately for the job – no loose hair, dangling neckties, or jewelry, no flapping cuffs or loose clothes. A guide and simple solution is to wear a hat, and to have a workshop coat with button-up cuffs.

Safety glasses

Safety goggles

31 EYE PROTECTION

Woodshops are inherently dangerous – fast-spinning machines, fragments of wood flying through the air, tools and machines that have the potential to fail catastrophically, and all the rest. You must wear protective glasses or a full-face mask. Don't think you can cut costs by using items like swimming goggles, because they can shatter into sharp-edged splinters. Get yourself a pair of approved safety glasses – and use them!

32 **EAR PROTECTION** High speed woodworking machines can be incredibly noisy. For example, some portable planers are so noisy that five minutes running time will leave your ears ringing and you feeling generally numbed and confused. It follows that you need to be wearing ear protection. To make ear protection even safer you should get a flashing light for the phone and work out hand signals so you can communicate with your woodshop buddy.

Ear defenders

Full face mask and respirator

33 **RESPIRATOR** The fine wood dust created by high speed machines is a hazard. The dust can result in breathing problems, skin rashes, dry eyes and all manner of health and safety delights. Dust is even more of a problem if you have it in mind to work with exotic tropical wood. Many woodworkers now wear helmet-mask type respirators. In use, the self-contained unit sucks air up through a filter and plays it down over your face to create a positive air environment. Yes, these respirators are expensive, but then again, they double up as eye protectors and some even offer ear protection. They can be worn over eye glasses, long hair, and whiskers.

Iroko

Afrormosia

Jelutong

European walnut

American red elm

American red oak

34 **TOXIC WOOD** Some woods are toxic – to the touch, to breathe in as dust, when they are in contact with some foods, when they are in contact with eye and nose membranes, and so on. If you are anxious about the notion, then the best safeguard is to follow approved health and safety recommendations as already described, and then have a policy of only using traditional tried and tested varieties.

LIFTING, MOVING, AND HOLDING EQUIPMENT

Maybe you are strong enough to lift and heave just about anything and everything that your woodshop is going to throw at you, but what's the point? Woodshop skills are not about gut-heaving feats of strength. Rather they have to do with being able to skillfully and efficiently perform all the tasks with the minimum of sweat and tears. The following tips will show you the best way forward.

35

BENDING AND LIFTING

When you come to lifting a heavy chunk of wood like a big turning blank or a small log from floor level, squat down, with your knees together, throw your arms around its middle – as if you were cuddling your mom – and then straighten your legs nice and easy.

BE WARNED – if you stoop over a heavy item, and try to lift it with a loose, belly-sagging, knees-apart, curved-back action, then you are asking for problems. If your work requires lots of lifting or bending, consider wearing a back support belt for extra protection against injury.

36

LIFTING BOARDS

When you are lifting heavy man-made boards up from the floor to the bench – say a ¼-inch thick sheet of plywood, particleboard or MDF – you most certainly put yourself at risk if you try to do it on your own. If you are a one-man band – or even a one-woman band – strap it with a flat webbing to make a handle, stand in a well-braced upright position, and use a controlled lift-and-slide action to ease it up onto the bench.

Adjust the straps so that the point-of-lift is at a comfortable height.

HAND TRUCK A small combination dolly or hand truck is a wonderfully efficient low-cost piece of safe-to-use equipment – perfect for moving small heavy items like bits of machinery and various logs and short lengths of lumber. A good money-saver is to go for one of the old-fashioned wood and steel type dollies that were traditionally used for moving very heavy weights like beer barrels and bags of sand. These can often be purchased easily second hand.

A flatbed truck enables you to move heavy loads with the minimum of effort.

SAWHORSES Fold-up sawhorses are primarily used for supporting materials that are too large for your bench. You could manage with a couple of old wooden crates or an upright chair, but a folding sawhorse is manageable and easy to store. Save money and make your own. Aim for a closed-up height of about 36 inches.

Tressels and sawhorses are invaluable around the workshop.

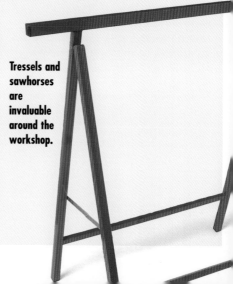

A matched pair of sawhorses makes for a safe sawing set-up.

39 **FEED ROLLERS** If you repeatedly need another pair of hands to help you support and guide stock into a machine or across a bench, then maybe you ought to consider getting yourself a pair of feed rollers. In use, the rollers are mounted on stands at the height of the work surface, and then simply located in line so that the stock is supported – like a conveyor belt. Feed rollers are a great way of reducing the risk of machine kick-back and/or jamming – when the sagging workpiece goes out of control. Feed rollers come in two types: One is a typical cylindrical roller, the other is made up of a line of rolling balls. The ball-type has the advantage of letting stock move in any direction across its surface.

Roller stand

40 **CLAMPS** Generally speaking, woodworkers need a lot of clamps – C-clamps, pipe clamps, bar clamps, and all the rest. Save money by buying only the sizes and types to suit the job at hand, then you won't be wasting your cash on a clamp that's never going to be used. Being mindful that C-clamps are sometimes used in potentially dangerous situations, only buy clamps that are forged.
BE WARNED – Cheap cast iron clamps are a bad idea, because they can fail catastrophically – with lots of sharp edges, and with the workpiece springing back out of control.

Quality C-Clamp

LIFTING, MOVING, AND HOLDING EQUIPMENT

41 **REACHING** It doesn't matter how tall or short you are: If you are stretching and reaching, then you are doing it wrong. Not only is there the potential for falling or damaging your back, but if machines are involved, the hazards increase. Stretching to control a workpiece on a table saw, for example, could very quickly bring you in contact with the saw blade. If you repeatedly find yourself stretching or reaching, then ask yourself why. Is the shelf too high? Is the bench too wide? Is the walk-around space restricted? Then solve the problem by getting a pair of steps, or lowering the shelf, or whatever seems appropriate.

42 **LEVERS AND ROLLERS** Who ever said, "Give me a lever long enough, and I will move the moon" – was it Archimedes? – certainly knew what he was talking about. If for example, you want to move a dead weight – you know, something like a table saw or lathe – from one side of the room to the other, then using wooden rollers and a length of lumber for a lever is the safe, sure answer.

BE WARNED – never be tempted to use metal-on-metal – meaning a metal bar to lever a cast iron machine. If you do, then you risk fracturing the iron.

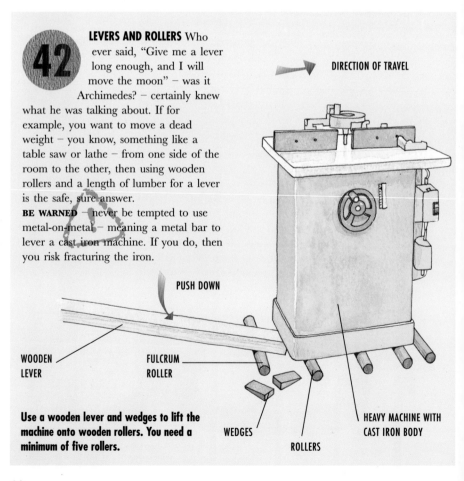

DIRECTION OF TRAVEL

PUSH DOWN

WOODEN LEVER

FULCRUM ROLLER

WEDGES

ROLLERS

HEAVY MACHINE WITH CAST IRON BODY

Use a wooden lever and wedges to lift the machine onto wooden rollers. You need a minimum of five rollers.

USING HAND TOOLS

Woodworking, whether it be carpentry, woodturning, carving or whatever, is to a great extent a simple matter of cutting and shaping wood with traditional sharp-edge hand tools. Tools like the saw, adze, axe, plane, chisel, gouge and knife are all basic to woodworking. So it logically follows that a good part of woodshop safety has to do with being able to use such edge tools with the minimum of effort. The following pointers will show you how to use and care for the primary cutting tools.

43 **CHISELS** Of all your hand tools, the chisels are, at one and the same time, the most widely used, the most open to abuse, and the most vulnerable. If you have a choice and are buying new, go for hand forged laminated steel blades, with fully honed ready-to-use cutting edges. The laminated steel will hold an edge longer. The guards that are usually supplied with the tools are designed to protect both you and the cutting edges – so don't lose them. Store chisels at a low level – never high up on a shelf where they are hard to reach and might fall, potentially damaging both you and their fine cutting edges.

Work with a safe two-handled cut – one hand pushing and the other holding and guiding.

When the job is done, protect the razor sharp bevel edge with a plastic guard.

44 **GOUGES** Carving is currently one of the fast growing woodcrafts, so even if you don't carve now, you will most likely eventually purchase and use one or more gouges. If you are a raw beginner and worried about safety, you won't go far wrong if you stay with these three rules of thumb:

● Always have the workpiece well supported with a clamp or bench holdfast.
● Always use a braced two-handed grip.
● Always cut away from your body.

1. Secure the workpiece with a clamp or bench stop.

2. Hold the tool with two hands and work at a low skimming angle. Use the guiding hand to fine-tune the cut.

45 **AXES AND ADZES**

Axes and adzes are commonly perceived as being not only anachronisms in a modern woodshop but difficult and dangerous tools to use. But if they are used with care and caution, they are both efficient and safe. Be mindful that the working height is critical, and the pendulum action is such, that it's not easy to stop the motion once the swing is under way. Set yourself up with a selection of log-section cutting blocks – so that you can always choose a safe working height to suit the task in hand.

BE WARNED – As older kids like the notion of axes and adzes, first show them how they are correctly used. This diminishes the forbidden-naughty-but-nice dynamics that some kids get into. Then be sure to store the tools under lock and key.

46 **KNIVES** The knife is often taken for granted, but one look over the average woodshop will confirm that it is still a primary tool. In use – mostly in carving – knives are wonderfully safe, as long as they are maneuvered, either with a braced two-handed away-from-the-body cut, or with a single-handed thumb-braced apple-paring cut. And, don't forget, a sharp knife is much safer to use than a blunt one that has to be forced through the work.

The levering action controls the cut.

47 **PLANES** Although portable power planers are showing up in more shops, hand planes are still the first-choice tool for making wood straight, flat, square and smooth. It's amazing how many woodworkers have plane-related accidents – damage to the workpiece, bloody knuckles, or bruised toes. First and foremost, the workpiece must be held securely, either in the vise, or with a hold-down. Secondly, in use, you need to make sure that the hand holding the body of the plane is positioned so that you don't get splinters or friction burns. Lastly, as planes are both heavy and relatively fragile, keep them away from the edge of the bench. A bruised toe and a cracked plane – what a mistake!

Secure the workpiece in the vise.

Make sure that your hands are in control and out of harm's way.

48

SAWS Most hand-saw accidents have to do with bad storage, or with blade slipping when the cut is being initiated. The first problem is easily solved: All you do is cover the teeth with a guard – a plastic strip or a wrap of old cloth – and be sure to store the saw where it can be seen and effortlessly reached. To avoid blade slipping, the safest procedure for starting a cut is to make a series of small dragging strokes until the teeth have made their mark. Rusty, blunt saws invariably jump and slip. Thus it follows that you won't go far wrong on the safety front if you always keep the blade sharp and rust free.

Handsaw

Do not use the tip of your thumb to guide the saw blade.

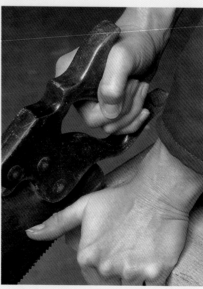

Use the heel of your thumb to steady the blade.

49 DRILLING Most drilling accidents have to do with the workpiece spinning off out of control to do damage to itself and anything that happens to be in its trajectory. Avoid such mishaps by being sure to clamp the workpiece down whenever possible. For clean, flat-bottom holes in wood, use Forstner type bits.

50 TOOL HANDLES A badly designed or broken tool handle inevitably results in a poor grip, and a poor grip causes friction and fatigue damage to your hands. All of that adds up to an accident in the making. Always make a point of ensuring that all handles – especially axes, adzes, chisels and gouges – are comfortable to hold and well fixed.

When using Forstner drill bits, a build-up of shavings in the hole can cause the bit to jam in the workpiece. For best results, use a slow drill speed and more than one plunge.

Damaged tool handles

Flat bits must be used at high speed to minimize wander and chatter. Avoid using bits with bent shanks as the vibration will dislodge the workpiece.

USING MACHINES

Modern woodworking machines are a joy – they are relatively inexpensive, easy-to-use, efficient, and generally safe. That said, if accidents do occur, they can be extremely serious – even life threatening. You must keep your machines in peak condition; you must read the manuals supplied with the machines; and you must take reasonable care. The following tips will show you how.

51 **ROUTERS** Many router accidents relate to poor control. The router rotates at very high speeds – much faster than most power tools. A variable speed router allows you to hold back on the power until you are just about to make contact with the workpiece and then match the power to the job at hand. This procedure ensures that you are the master – not the tool! It's vital that you always feed your work in the correct direction – against rather than with the spin of the router bit. Otherwise the bit may slip and skate along the workpiece. Check with the manual and the cutter head type, and follow the recommendations for your machine.

A hand held router needs to be used with care and caution.

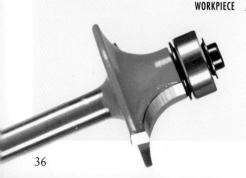

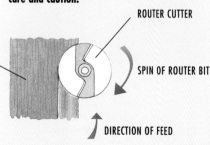

WORKPIECE

ROUTER CUTTER

SPIN OF ROUTER BIT

DIRECTION OF FEED

Note the direction of spin in relationship to the direction of feed.

SHAPERS

The shaper is one of the most dangerous machines in your workshop simply because it's difficult to guard against the fast-spinning cutter. Your best line of positive defense is to familiarize yourself with the direction of spin – it might even be reversible – and then set up jigs and side tables, so that you can feed the workpiece with a steady strong hand and maximum control. Use of zero-clearance auxiliary fences, anti-kickback fingers and push sticks all add to safety.

Never work with the guard in the "up" position.

Adjust the guard height shields so that they fit the size of the workpiece.

POWER CARVER A power carver can be anything from a high-tech tool with a reciprocating gouge head or a sophisticated rotary tool that can carve in miniature, through to a large angle grinder or even a router-type option fitted onto a power drill. Regardless of the variations, the overall dangers have to do with dust, noise, and hand control. Always secure the workpiece in a vise or with a holdfast, and always wear goggles and a respirator. **BE WARNED** – a hot tool or shaft is an early warning that the bearings need re-greasing and/or the air feed is choked with dust.

MACHINES IN MOTION
Many accidents have to do with not appreciating that such-and-such a quiet-running machine is actually in motion. A low-cost solution is to apply a dash of color to wheels and other moving parts, so as to create a flicker-warning when the machine is in action.

BAND SAW GUIDE The safety function of the band saw blade guide is two-fold – the lowered guard stops you from accidentally touching the blade, while at the same time the guides and bearings at the back of the guard help keep the blade in line and prevent catastrophic blade failure. Always lower the guard to permit just sufficient clearance of the workpiece under the guard. That will ensure maximum support for the blade as well as maximum safety for you.

1. Adjust the guide so that the back edge of the blade is supported.

2. Align the runners so that the blade is centralized.

3. Fine-tune the wheel-stop so that there is a slight clearance at the back edge of the blade.

4. Adjust the height of the guide/guard so that it is about ½ inch clear of the workpiece.

56 **LATHE CHUCK** Though a four-jaw chuck is one of the best ways of securing the workpiece, there is the danger that you will brush your left arm or hand up against the protruding jaws of the chuck while the lathe is in motion. An inexpensive guard can be made by bending a sheet of ⅛-inch-thick plywood in a curve, and fixing it in place with a couple of C-clamps – so that it bridges the chuck.

The easy-to-make guard protects your left arm from the spinning chuck.

57 **CAST IRON TABLES** If your machine table surfaces become so gummed up that they require a great deal of effort to keep the workpiece moving, then they are most certainly dangerous. The simplest safety action is to first clean off the resin with a fine emery cloth, then clean the surface with a solvent soaked cloth, and finally polish the whole surface with one or other of the graphite anti-friction products that are on the market.

58 **MACHINE VIBRATION** If you find that one of your cast iron machine stands develops a potentially dangerous vibration, first check for loose parts or adjustments. If you find the cause is an uneven floor, the easiest and cheapest solution is to level it with a wedge. This is achieved by first cutting a hardwood wedge and a piece of ¼-inch-thick plywood. Smear glue over mating faces on the plywood and the wedge. Then tap them in place at the base. When the glue is set, use an old saw or chisel to cut the wood back flush with the machine.

DEBRIS COLLECTION AND CLEANLINESS

Wood dust not only harms the lungs, clogs the machines, and is a fire risk, it also has the potential to creep from the shop environment back to home and hearth. As for all the offcuts, disposal is an ever-pressing chore. There is clearly a correlation between cleanliness and safety. The following tips will show you the way.

59

DUST COLLECTION According to the Occupational Safety and Health Administration (OSHA) you should limit your exposure to fine wood dust. In very broad terms, they suggest that if you were to puff a heaped teaspoon of dust into the average garage-size woodshop and then spend more than fifteen minutes a day in this atmosphere, you would be exceeding safe limits. For safety's sake, you need to stay with the following rules of thumb:

- Cut down on the amount of dust at source – by using filtered machines, and/or by producing shavings rather than dust.
- Capture as much dust as possible by using a vacuum system.
- Wear a dustmask/respirator.

Make sure that all your small power tools are fitted with dust bags.

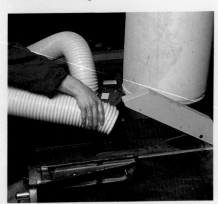

Use a mobile dust vacuum system to service individual machines.

Be mindful that tools are easily lost amid floor shavings.

A buildup of debris can easily impede the safe running of a machine.

Be warned – a buildup of sawdust and machine oil is a dangerous mix!

60 DEBRIS COLLECTION
Woodshop debris, in the form of shavings and offcuts scattered around on the floor, is a dangerous nuisance. On the one hand the shavings will polish the floor to the extent that it becomes slippery, and on the other hand, loose offcuts can easily be tripped over. It's good woodshop practice to make a point of sorting the debris into stuff that can be used for small projects, bits that might be recycled into, say, dowels and such like and pieces that need to be thrown away.

BITS AND PIECES FOR SMALL PROJECTS

LONG PIECES

OFF-CUTS

SAWDUST

Organize your debris collection for maximum efficiency – bags for dust, garbage cans for fragments, and racks and boxes for reusable off-cuts.

DEBRIS COLLECTION AND CLEANLINESS

61 **STOVES** More and more, woodworkers are coming around to the idea, that perhaps the best user-friendly option for disposing of wood waste – dust and off-cuts – is to burn it in a super-efficient woodburning stove. With the opportunity for a dry atmosphere for the tools, a clean floor AND warm fingers, nose, and toes, a woodburner is a great money-saving idea. However, make sure that it is installed properly according to local fire and building codes. Otherwise, your friendly woodstove may introduce a serious fire hazard to your shop.

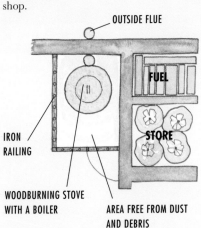

OUTSIDE FLUE

FUEL

STORE

IRON
RAILING

WOODBURNING STOVE
WITH A BOILER

AREA FREE FROM DUST
AND DEBRIS

Ring the woodburning stove off behind a metal railing or caging.

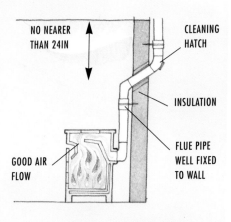

NO NEARER
THAN 24IN

CLEANING
HATCH

INSULATION

GOOD AIR
FLOW

FLUE PIPE
WELL FIXED
TO WALL

Be sure to follow installation safety codes.

62 **OILY RAGS** Oily rags – meaning rags soaked in motor oil, solvents, French polish, spar varnish, linseed oil, brush cleaner and such like – are dangerous. Under certain warm-and-enclosed conditions, the rags can smolder and spontaneously combust. Remove the rags from your workshop as soon as you have finished with them. Wet them down and put them into a metal garbage can. On no account drop the rags into a plastic wastebasket, or seal them up in a plastic bag, as this can increase the risk of fume build-up and fire. Special air-tight metal cans are available for temporary rag disposal.

PET LITTER If you do decide to use your shavings and wood dust as pet litter – say bedding for your rabbits, or a tray for your cat, or whatever – then you must remember, that the fine dust is just as harmful for your pets as it is for yourself.

NAILS A vast number of very painful woodshop accidents have to do with woodworkers stepping on nails – meaning nails that have been hammered through a bit of wood, and then left around on the floor. The best defence is to remove the nail or scrap wood. If you are too busy, at least hammer the nail over so that it doesn't stick up.

1. Never leave nail-spiked off-cuts sitting around on the floor.

2. Remove nails with a claw hammer and wear thick soled safety boots – just in case you miss a nail!

3. If you are short of time, then swiftly hammer the nails over and go back to them another day.

MAINTENANCE OF TOOLS

There is an old woodworking adage that asserts that a swift, sharp blade is a good deal safer than a slow, dull one. If you find that your cutting edges need to be forced into action, it is a sure indicator that you and the tools are at risk. The following tips will show you how to sharpen and care for your cutting edges, and in so doing make your woodshop safer and more efficient.

Hold the tool flat down on the rest and adjust the shield so that your eyes are protected from sparks and fragments.

65 **GRINDING** The sharpening sequence – from first to last – goes grinding, honing, and stropping. Remember, you only really need to resort to grinding if your chisel or whatever has been damaged or neglected. If your tool needs grinding, make sure you use a tool rest to properly maintain the correct bevel angle. A slow-moving grindstone is the safest and most foolproof way to grind a bevel. It allows you time to customize and shape the tool with little risk to your hand or the steel. If you must use a high-speed bench grinder, be careful not to overheat the steel. Quench the tool often in water and don't apply too much pressure. Of course, always wear a face shield or safety glasses.

Well-maintained edge

Damaged and poorly ground edge

Angle the tool so that the primary bevel is in contact and then lift the handle slightly so as to achieve the cutting bevel.

66 **HONING** Honing is the post-grinding procedure of rubbing the bevel edges on a series of graded stones. The object is first to remove the deep scratches on the coarse stone, and then to polish the metal to a finer and finer finish. Again, be careful to maintain the correct bevel angle. A number of special fixtures are available to help hold the tool at the right sharpening angle. Being mindful that the honed tool is razor sharp, be sure to store it in a safe place when the job is done.

BE WARNED – in the knowledge that fine wisps of waste metal are very dangerous – they can easily pierce the skin and get in your eyes – always lubricate the stone (oil stones with honing oil and water stones with water) to hold the waste down, and maintain the stone's efficiency. Wipe up when you have finished.

When honing large blades, be careful not to slip off the edge of the sharpening stone.

67 **STROPPING** The final and finest procedure in the sharpening sequence is stropping. The purpose of the exercise is to polish the cutting edge to the shiniest of shiny finishes, and to remove the fine wisp of waste metal – the wire – that clings to the edge of the bevel. Remember, that while stropped tools are safe in use – because they get the job done swiftly and cleanly – they are also dangerous in the wrong hands. If you have kids, be sure to store the tools in a safe place.

HAMMERS If you have a hammer with a loose head or a split handle – or even an axe or adze come to that – then either get a new one, or spend time fixing it. Drive another wedge into the top of the head, or fit a replacement handle.

FILES A file with a loose handle, or no handle, is a dangerous menace – more a weapon than a woodworking tool. Some woodworkers grind old files to shape and use them for lathe tools, but be mindful that when a file shatters catastrophically, it throws out a shower of sharp-edge fragments. Never use a file without a handle. To fit a wooden handle to a file, first grip the blade in a padded vise, and then tap the handle home with a hammer or wooden mallet. Do not hit the file blade.

Never use a file without a handle.

Be sure to tap the handle onto the blade – never the other way around.

70 **RUST** Rust is a two-fold problem: It not only damages tools and machines – and so consequently makes them potentially unsafe – it also stains the wood. As the underside of metal planes, and cutting blades, and such like can't be painted, many woodworkers advocate a generous dusting with baby powder/talc. The thinking is, that the powder not only displaces moisture, it also serves as a good lubricant between the wood and the tool/machine. If you keep your woodshop dry and well ventilated, you shouldn't have any problems.

1. Use a fine-grade wire wool to remove rust.

2. Be mindful that when you clean the plane sole, you must use an even allover stroke.

3. Protect the now clean metal with a film of fine engine oil.

71 **LUBRICATION** Lubrication needs to be near the top of your safety check list. Machine surfaces occasionally need to be wiped over with thin oil or wax, moving machine parts need to be lubricated according to the user's manual, in certain instances the undersides of metal hand planes need to be wiped over with oil or wax, and so on. If you hear squeaks and groans when you power up a machine, then the chances are it needs proper lubrication. Just remember: If a moving part is badly in need of lubrication, then it might fail catastrophically!

Having lubricated the moving parts – spray the work table with wax polish so as to achieve a low friction surface.

FINISHING

Though wood finishing can be a wonderfully satisfying activity – when you can at last see a project coming together – it is also an operation that is fraught with potential dangers, not the least of which are poisonous fumes, toxic liquids, flammable and corrosive substances. The good news is that most finishing accidents can be easily prevented simply by avoiding such sloppy woodshop procedures as not reading labels and leaving adhesives and such just sitting around on the work surfaces. Such pitfalls can easily be side-stepped. The following tips will show you how.

72 SMOKING Do not smoke in the woodshop. No matter how careful you are, the wood dust or shavings might catch fire, or flammable finishes might ignite, or a cigarette butt might fall behind a bench, and so on. Smoking and woodshops are a bad mix! Put up NO SMOKING signs so that visitors get the message clearly.

73 SANDING When you come to sanding, position the dust collector or shop vacuum so that the hose inlet is nicely placed over the working area. For convenience, you can design a flex-arm arrangement, so that the machine can be quickly relocated.

Be aware that all wood dust is potentially toxic.

74 ALLERGIC REACTIONS

If you find yourself sneezing, or coming up with a skin rash, or your nose is running, then you need either to go for another wood type or finish or you need to reconsider your body protection arrangements. Many woodworkers opt for wearing latex gloves and disposable cover-alls.

If your power tool isn't fitted with a dust collector, then use a mobile shop vacuum.

75 **FINISHES** In the push toward making woodshops safer, woodworkers are more and more advocating the use of non-toxic, low-odor, non-flammable water-based paints, stains, and varnishes. Note that some states have specific restrictions that limit the use of traditional finishes like spirit varnish. If you are employing people and are ignorant about toxic finishes and such like, then contact your local OSHA representative and ask for advice. You should also obtain copies of Material Safety and Data Sheets (MSDS) from the manufacturers of products you use.

76 **PAINTING AREA** If you have it in mind to do a lot of woodwork, then it's best if you organize a small, clean dust-free area that is set aside for finishing. You could either screen off some part of the woodshop and provide it with positive ventilation – so that air tracks from the painting area to the outside – or you could go for a totally separate room. Any fan used in a spray finishing area should be of the explosion-proof variety.

A spray gun needs to be used with great care and caution.

77 **TOXIC WASTE** If and when you come to dispose of toxic waste materials, like old paint, or waste motor oil, or leftovers of adhesive, or whatever, first store them outside the workshop in a clearly labeled metal bin, and then seek the advice of your local health and safety department for proper disposal. Be mindful that it's not a good idea to mix chemicals.

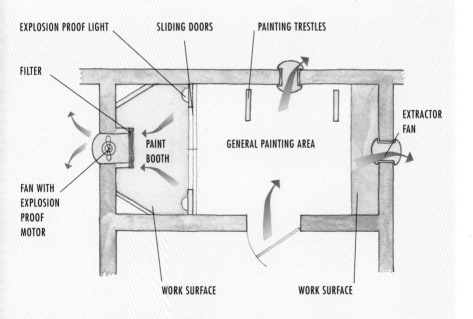

EXPLOSION PROOF LIGHT

SLIDING DOORS

PAINTING TRESTLES

FILTER

EXTRACTOR FAN

PAINT BOOTH

GENERAL PAINTING AREA

FAN WITH EXPLOSION PROOF MOTOR

WORK SURFACE

WORK SURFACE

Set an area aside for brush and spray painting.

WHAT TO DO IN AN EMERGENCY

Okay, so you run the cleanest, tidiest woodshop on the block, and you have put every single safeguard in place. But what if? What are you going to do if there is an emergency? On the premise that it's much better to be prepared, the following guides will show you how to set up a positive emergency program – just in case!

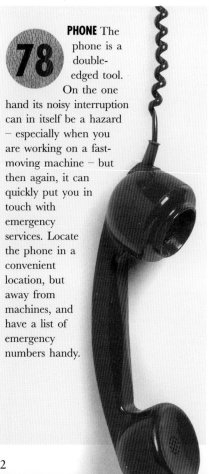

78 **PHONE** The phone is a double-edged tool. On the one hand its noisy interruption can in itself be a hazard – especially when you are working on a fast-moving machine – but then again, it can quickly put you in touch with emergency services. Locate the phone in a convenient location, but away from machines, and have a list of emergency numbers handy.

79 **WORK PROGRAM** You don't want to be left in some sort of home-alone nightmare – bleeding, trapped on the floor, with your finger caught. That's why it's a good idea to always tell friends and family what you are doing, and just how long you intend to be in the woodshop. You could have a positive policy of telling your nearest and dearest just how long you are going to be working – like a pilot tells his estimated time of arrival.

80 **EYE INJURIES** If you get something in your eye, do not rub the eye, or rub the lid over the eye, or poke around with a toothpick or use an eye cup. Simply hold a sterile dressing over the closed eye with a band aid, and immediately go to a doctor or hospital emergency room. DO NOT DRIVE – get a friend or helper to do the driving.

81 **CUTS AND SPLINTERS** If you have a woodshop, then its only a matter of time before you scrape a knuckle, or cut your finger on a chisel, or run a splinter up your finger nail or whatever. It's a good idea to be ready with a well-stocked first aid kit. You need bandages, gauze, a pair of scissors, a pair of tweezers, a sterilized needle, and a tube/bottle of antiseptic to rub on the wound.

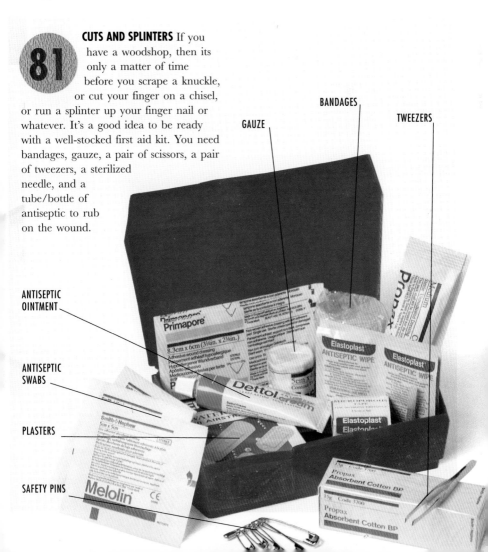

BANDAGES

GAUZE

TWEEZERS

ANTISEPTIC OINTMENT

ANTISEPTIC SWABS

PLASTERS

SAFETY PINS

WHAT TO DO IN AN EMERGENCY

82

FIRST AID CHART An accident like a nasty gash to the hand or a crushed finger is not uncommon in the woodshop. This being the case, you should display a basic first aid chart on the wall, familiarize yourself with recommended first aid practices, and list the emergency phone numbers of your nearest doctor or hospital emergency room.

FIRE BLANKET   FIRE CHART

FIRE EXTINGUISHERS

WATER   SAND

Make sure that your fire extinguishers are in good condition and easy to reach.

83

FIRE EXTINGUISHERS Every woodshop should have at least one fire extinguisher of the dry powder type, a bucket of water, a bucket of sand, and a fire blanket. In an emergency, like, say, an electrical glue pot bursting into flame, you should first of all turn off the power, and then control the fire with the sand and/or the extinguisher. On no account should you start throwing the water around onto live machinery. For even more protection, position extinguishers at different points around the shop.

Check that your extinguishers can be used on electrical fires.

84 **EMERGENCY EXITS** Your woodshop must have, at the very least, two exits – say an unobstructed door, and a large opening window. If you are working upstairs, then you also need to plan a suitable fire escape. If you are employing help – even on a part-time basis – then you must follow recommended guidelines. If you have any doubts, seek the advice of your local health and safety department.

Clean the dust and dirt from the inside of the smoke alarm.

85 **SMOKE ALARMS** If you are anxious about fire risks – and this is perhaps more of a problem if your woodshop is an integral part of your home – then smoke alarms are a must. They are a swift, sure, money-saving means of detecting smoke. The average large-garage size woodshop should have three alarms – one at the center of the room, one farthest away from the door, and one nearest the door.

86 **SEVERED FINGERS** Okay, so it's not a pleasant notion – but it is a possibility, and accidents do happen! A current magazine article tells how, when a woodworker cut three of his fingers off on the band saw, he bound his hand up with a towel to stop the blood, packed the fingers in a box with frozen fish sticks and then drove to the hospital where the fingers were successfully sewn back on. Apparently, what saved the fingers was the fact that they were frozen. Just remember: Frozen fingers are better than no fingers!

87 **ELECTRICAL SHOCK** In case of electrical shock – when the accident victim is holding the cable, tool or whatever – the first thing to do is to turn off the power. This should be swiftly followed up with a phone call to the emergency services, wrapping the victim up in a blanket, and making sure the mouth is clear of obstructions.

BE WARNED – resuscitation techniques need to be done with care and caution. Follow the advice as shown on your emergency chart.

If your power tool looks like this little beauty – a ragged flex and bits of tape – then switch off the power and have the tool overhauled.

88 **SEVERE BLEEDING** When arteries are cut or a number of veins have been lacerated, severe bleeding will occur – usually in bright red spurts. The first aid provider – this might even be the victim himself/herself – should immediately locate the source of the pumping blood, and then apply finger pressure or whole-hand pressure with a sterile gauze or towel to stop the flow.

SPECIFIC MACHINE TOOL SAFETY

Not so long ago, the average small woodshop had a table saw, maybe a drill press and a router, and that was about it. All the other tasks were performed with hand tools. Now of course, most woodshops are chock-a-block with all manner of powerful fast-running efficient machines – everything from lathes, band saws, planers, jointers, power carvers and scroll saws, through to bench saws, chain saws, shapers and sanders. There's no denying that machines pose the biggest safety problems, if only because, when machine accidents do occur, they tend to be swift and catastrophic. The best overall advice – having first read the user manual – is never to work on a machine until you have a clear understanding as to its function, and to always keep machines well maintained. The following machine-specific tips will help you run a safe and efficient woodshop.

If your workpiece is short, then be sure to use push sticks. Never put your hands at risk.

89 **TABLE SAW** If you intend to rip a long length on a table saw, you must use the machine in conjunction with an outfeed table and hold-downs. The outfeed table minimizes problems involved with wood kickback and binding, and the hold-down stops the workpiece from rising off the worktable to the point where it is thrown back like a javelin. Always wear safety glasses, always use push sticks, and always make sure that the push-sticks stay away from the blades. Not forgetting that, if the wood chatters and starts to split, then it might split off and shoot backwards like a spear. Always stand well to one side of the line of feed.

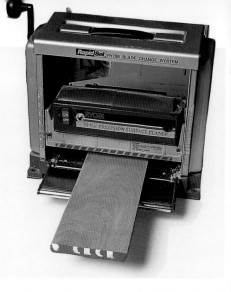

PORTABLE PLANER

90 A portable planer is a wonderfully efficient tool – perfect for the small woodshop. Having protected yourself against the dust and the noise, the main hazards have to do with feed and kick-back. The primary no-no's are: never try to plane a piece shorter than about 12 inches, never stand directly behind the machine, never force the rate of feed, and never let small children anywhere near when the machine is up and running.

BAND SAW Though the band saw is one of the most efficient woodworking machines going, its very efficiency tends to lull the woodworker into thinking that it can be used with careless abandon – like a food mixer. No way! A current magazine likens the band saw to a quiet beast that is just waiting to nip your fingers off. The good news is that bird's-mouth push sticks can be swiftly and easily made in just a few minutes – a great money-saving safety aid! In use, the push sticks are held like eating irons, and used to feed and guide the workpiece through the machine. Always lower the upper blade guide so as little of the blade is exposed as possible.

1. When working with a long length of wood, use your hands to start the cut.

Scroll saws are uniquely safe – perfect for anxious beginners.

92 **SCROLL SAW** If you are a nervous beginner to woodwork, and you have it in mind to cut fancy curves and profiles in thin wood – say hand-size pieces up to 1¼ inches thick – then the scroll saw is the machine for you. This machine is just about as safe and foolproof as you can get. Its uniquely high safety record is borne out by the fact that the scroll saw is one of the few woodworking machines allowed in schools for young kids.

2. When the end of the workpiece comes to within 6 inches of the blade, use a pair of push sticks.

3. When you come to finish, reduce the rate of cut, and reposition the push sticks for optimum control.

Use a brush, cloth, and mineral spirits to clean away the buildup of resin. The shanks need to be bright and free from pits and steel-burn.

93 **ROUTER** A router is a great tool for cutting slots and profiles, and for producing moldings – a real must for the small woodshop. The main accidents and mess-ups with the router have to do with leaving the bit in place, and with not cleaning up the dust and resin once the job is done. The gradual build-up results in wear and bit slippage. Don't be tempted to polish the shank or the collet with steel wool, as repeated cleanings will make for a loose and sloppy fit. Simply wipe it with mineral spirits and a thin smear of light oil.

94 **LATHE** If and when you find that you need a lathe, get yourself the biggest and best that you can afford. In use, the lathe is a relatively safe and user-friendly machine, as long as you follow a few rules. Always make sure that your clothes and hair are tied back before you switch on the power. Always work with long-handled tools. And always make sure that the workpiece is totally secure. As the most common accidents have to do with the workpiece flying off, you must always wear goggles, or better yet, an all-over face visor-respirator. If you are really nervous, you could fit a safety shield in front of the machine.

Aim for a lathe that has big, bold, positive stay-put controls and a heavy vibration-free structure.

A selection of router cutters that have seen a
lot of hard use. These can be cleaned up and
honed by hand or completely re-sharpened.

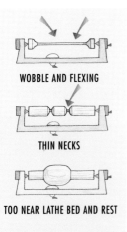

WOBBLE AND FLEXING

THIN NECKS

TOO NEAR LATHE BED AND REST

OFF-CENTER
DAMAGES
BEARINGS

95 **PLATE JOINER** A portable plate or biscuit joiner is a good tool – a valuable addition to most woodshops. In essence, it cuts slots or kerfs in such a way that mating pieces of wood can be butted and joined together by means of a thin plate of compressed wood called a biscuit. In use, accidents have to do with the workpiece shifting, and/or the tool bucking. The two primary safety points to stay with are to spend plenty of time securing the workpiece and to make sure that the anti-kickback pins are in contact with the wood to be slotted.

**Biscuit joint
insert**

BAND SAW BLADES

96 When you buy a new band saw blade, it will be tightly coiled up on itself – a bit like a spring. Being mindful that it will bounce open the moment you undo the binding – a whole hoop of razor sharp teeth – the best procedure is to wear gloves and a face mask. Then unwrap the blade in an open area by tossing it out away from you on the floor, where it can harmlessly spring back to its natural shape.

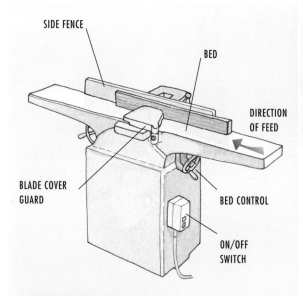

SIDE FENCE

BED

DIRECTION OF FEED

BLADE COVER GUARD

BED CONTROL

ON/OFF SWITCH

A small combination planer-jointer

97 **SURFACE PLANER** The surface planer is the fastest and most accurate way to achieve truly square sides and edges on your lumber, but the jointer is also one of the most dangerous machines in the woodshop. Always keep guards in place and be careful to keep fingers away from the cutterhead. Use push sticks and push blocks to guide the work past the cutterhead. Do not joint pieces shorter than 12 inches.

98 **DRILL PRESS** Although the bench drill press has a pretty good safety record, the fact that it is used at chest and face level does put you at special risk. Long hair, loose clothing or jewelry are all a hazard. The drill press's small table also presents a problem when drilling large workpieces. Make sure large pieces are properly supported and clamped.

If you are working with a drill bit larger than ½ inch diameter, then be sure to hold the workpiece in a clamp/vise.

99 **MACHINE MOMENTUM** Most wood-working machines carry on moving even after switch-off, so you mustn't be tempted to stop the blade or chuck with your hands. Use a length of scrap wood instead.

100 **MACHINE LOCATION** A really good money-saving tip for securing machines and benches to the floor – so that they stay put, don't wobble, and are safe – is first to wedge them to the corrrect height with thin shims of wood, then use a glue gun to run a bead around the base of the machine. When the glue is set, the little ridge will prevent the wedges from slipping out, and so prevent the machine from creeping.

CREDITS

Quarto Publishing would like to thank the following for their permission to reproduce copyright material: p6 Ercol Furniture, Buckinghamshire; p26 Image Bank.

All other photographs are the copyright of Quarto Publishing.

We would like to acknowledge and thank Axminster Power Tool Centre, Chard Street, Axminster, Devon, who very kindly loaned the tools and equipment featured in this book.

We would finally like to thank Tim Hodgkinson, Simone Oliver and Alan Thomas at Pendryn Furniture, 2b Barbican Industrial Estate, East Looe, Cornwall, who kindly permitted us to photograph at their premises.

Senior Art editor Penny Cobb
Designer Glyn Bridgewater
Photographers Ian Howes, Jeremy Thomas
Illustrator Gill Bridgewater
Text editor William Sampson
Senior editor Kate Kirby
Prop researcher Miriam Hyman
Picture manager Giulia Hetherington
Editorial director Mark Dartford
Art director Moira Clinch

Typeset by Genesis Typesetting, Rochester and
Central Southern Typesetters, Eastbourne
Manufactured by Bright Arts (Singapore) Pte Ltd.
Printed in China by Leefung-Asco Printers Ltd.